STUDENT PLANNER 2019-2020

STUDY PRINTY

THIS PLANNER BELONGS TO:

NAME:

BIRTHDAY:

ADDRESS:

PHONE:

EMAIL:

UNIVERSITY:

MY CONTACTS

NAME

ADDRESS

EMAIL

HANDY

NAME

ADDRESS

EMAIL

HANDY

NAME

ADDRESS

EMAIL

HANDY

NAME

ADDRESS

EMAIL

HANDY

NAME

ADDRESS

EMAIL

HANDY

NAME

ADDRESS

EMAIL

HANDY

NAME

ADDRESS

EMAIL

HANDY

NAME

ADDRESS

EMAIL

HANDY

NAME	
ADDRESS	
EMAIL	
HANDY	

NAME	
ADDRESS	
EMAIL	
HANDY	

NAME	
ADDRESS	
EMAIL	
HANDY	

NAME	
ADDRESS	
EMAIL	
HANDY	

NAME	
ADDRESS	
EMAIL	
HANDY	

NAME	
ADDRESS	
EMAIL	
HANDY	

NAME	
ADDRESS	
EMAIL	
HANDY	

NAME	
ADDRESS	
EMAIL	
HANDY	

MY CONTACTS

NAME

ADDRESS

EMAIL

HANDY

NAME

ADDRESS

EMAIL

HANDY

NAME

ADDRESS

EMAIL

HANDY

NAME

ADDRESS

EMAIL

HANDY

NAME

ADDRESS

EMAIL

HANDY

NAME

ADDRESS

EMAIL

HANDY

NAME

ADDRESS

EMAIL

HANDY

NAME

ADDRESS

EMAIL

HANDY

NAME		NAME	
ADDRESS		ADDRESS	
EMAIL		EMAIL	
HANDY		HANDY	

NAME		NAME	
ADDRESS		ADDRESS	
EMAIL		EMAIL	
HANDY		HANDY	

NAME		NAME	
ADDRESS		ADDRESS	
EMAIL		EMAIL	
HANDY		HANDY	

NAME		NAME	
ADDRESS		ADDRESS	
EMAIL		EMAIL	
HANDY		HANDY	

GOALS

 **BIRTHDAYS**

NAME	DATE	DATE	NAME

JAN 2019
MO	TU	WE	TH	FR	SA	SU
	1	2	3	4	5	6
7	8	9	10	11	12	13
14	15	16	17	18	19	20
21	22	23	24	25	26	27
28	29	30	31			

FEB 2019
MO	TU	WE	TH	FR	SA	SU
				1	2	3
4	5	6	7	8	9	10
11	12	13	14	15	16	17
18	19	20	21	22	23	24
25	26	27	28			

MAR 2019
MO	TU	WE	TH	FR	SA	SU
				1	2	3
4	5	6	7	8	9	10
11	12	13	14	15	16	17
18	19	20	21	22	23	24
25	26	27	28	29	30	31

APR 2019
MO	TU	WE	TH	FR	SA	SU
1	2	3	4	5	6	7
8	9	10	11	12	13	14
15	16	17	18	19	20	21
22	23	24	25	26	27	28
29	30					

MAY 2019
MO	TU	WE	TH	FR	SA	SU
		1	2	3	4	5
6	7	8	9	10	11	12
13	14	15	16	17	18	19
20	21	22	23	24	25	26
27	28	29	30	31		

JUN 2019
MO	TU	WE	TH	FR	SA	SU
					1	2
3	4	5	6	7	8	9
10	11	12	13	14	15	16
17	18	19	20	21	22	23
24	25	26	27	28	29	30

JUL 2019
MO	TU	WE	TH	FR	SA	SU
1	2	3	4	5	6	7
8	9	10	11	12	13	14
15	16	17	18	19	20	21
22	23	24	25	26	27	28
29	30	31				

AUG 2019
MO	TU	WE	TH	FR	SA	SU
			1	2	3	4
5	6	7	8	9	10	11
12	13	14	15	16	17	18
19	20	21	22	23	24	25
26	27	28	29	30	31	

SEPT 2019
MO	TU	WE	TH	FR	SA	SU
						1
2	3	4	5	6	7	8
9	10	11	12	13	14	15
16	17	18	19	20	21	22
23	24	25	26	27	28	29
30						

OCT 2019
MO	TU	WE	TH	FR	SA	SU
	1	2	3	4	5	6
7	8	9	10	11	12	13
14	15	16	17	18	19	20
21	22	23	24	25	26	27
28	29	30	31			

NOV 2019
MO	TU	WE	TH	FR	SA	SU
				1	2	3
4	5	6	7	8	9	10
11	12	13	14	15	16	17
18	19	20	21	22	23	24
25	26	27	28	29	30	

DEC 2019
MO	TU	WE	TH	FR	SA	SU
						1
2	3	4	5	6	7	8
9	10	11	12	13	14	15
16	17	18	19	20	21	22
23	24	25	26	27	28	29
30	31					

JAN 2020
MO	TU	WE	TH	FR	SA	SU
		1	2	3	4	5
6	7	8	9	10	11	12
13	14	15	16	17	18	19
20	21	22	23	24	25	26
27	28	29	30	31		

FEB 2020
MO	TU	WE	TH	FR	SA	SU
					1	2
3	4	5	6	7	8	9
10	11	12	13	14	15	16
17	18	19	20	21	22	23
24	25	26	27	28	29	

MAR 2020
MO	TU	WE	TH	FR	SA	SU
						1
2	3	4	5	6	7	8
9	10	11	12	13	14	15
16	17	18	19	20	21	22
23	24	25	26	27	28	29
30	31					

APR 2020
MO	TU	WE	TH	FR	SA	SU
		1	2	3	4	5
6	7	8	9	10	11	12
13	14	15	16	17	18	19
20	21	22	23	24	25	26
27	28	29	30			

MAY 2020
MO	TU	WE	TH	FR	SA	SU
				1	2	3
4	5	6	7	8	9	10
11	12	13	14	15	16	17
18	19	20	21	22	23	24
25	26	27	28	29	30	31

JUN 2020
MO	TU	WE	TH	FR	SA	SU
1	2	3	4	5	6	7
8	9	10	11	12	13	14
15	16	17	18	19	20	21
22	23	24	25	26	27	28
29	30					

JUL 2020
MO	TU	WE	TH	FR	SA	SU
		1	2	3	4	5
6	7	8	9	10	11	12
13	14	15	16	17	18	19
20	21	22	23	24	25	26
27	28	29	30	31		

AUG 2020
MO	TU	WE	TH	FR	SA	SU
					1	2
3	4	5	6	7	8	9
10	11	12	13	14	15	16
17	18	19	20	21	22	23
24	25	26	27	28	29	30
31						

SEPT 2020
MO	TU	WE	TH	FR	SA	SU
	1	2	3	4	5	6
7	8	9	10	11	12	13
14	15	16	17	18	19	20
21	22	23	24	25	26	27
28	29	30				

OCT 2020
MO	TU	WE	TH	FR	SA	SU
			1	2	3	4
5	6	7	8	9	10	11
12	13	14	15	16	17	18
19	20	21	22	23	24	25
26	27	28	29	30	31	

NOV 2020
MO	TU	WE	TH	FR	SA	SU
						1
2	3	4	5	6	7	8
9	10	11	12	13	14	15
16	17	18	19	20	21	22
23	24	25	26	27	28	29
30						

DEC 2020
MO	TU	WE	TH	FR	SA	SU
	1	2	3	4	5	6
7	8	9	10	11	12	13
14	15	16	17	18	19	20
21	22	23	24	25	26	27
28	29	30	31			

2019

2020

01	TH			01	SU	
02	FR			02	MO	Labor Day	36
03	SA			03	TU	
04	SU			04	WE	
05	MO	32		05	TH	
06	TU			06	FR	
07	WE			07	SA	
08	TH			08	SU	Grandparents Day
09	FR			09	MO	37
10	SA			10	TU	
11	SU			11	WE	Patriot Day
12	MO	33		12	TH	
13	TU			13	FR	
14	WE			14	SA	
15	TH			15	SU	
16	FR			16	MO	Step Family Day
17	SA			17	TU	Citizenship Day
18	SU			18	WE	
19	MO	34		19	TH	
20	TU			20	FR	
21	WE			21	SA	
22	TH			22	SU	
23	FR			23	MO	39
24	SA			24	TU	
25	SU			25	WE	
26	MO	35		26	TH	
27	TU			27	FR	Native American Day
28	WE			28	SA	
29	TH			29	SU	
30	FR			30	MO	40
31	SA					

OCTOBER			NOVEMBER		
01	TU		01	FR	
02	WE		02	SA	
03	TH		03	SU	Daylight Saving
04	FR		04	MO	45
05	SA		05	TU	
06	SU		06	WE	
07	MO	41	07	TH	
08	TU		08	FR	
09	WE		09	SA	
10	TH		10	SU	
11	FR		11	MO	Veterans Day 46
12	SA		12	TU	
13	SU		13	WE	
14	MO	Columbus Day 42	14	TH	
15	TU		15	FR	
16	WE	Boss Day	16	SA	
17	TH		17	SU	
18	FR		18	MO	47
19	SA	Sweetest Day	19	TU	
20	SU		20	WE	
21	MO	43	21	TH	
22	TU		22	FR	
23	WE		23	SA	
24	TH		24	SU	
25	FR		25	MO	48
26	SA		26	TU	
27	SU		27	WE	
28	MO	44	28	TH	Thanksgiving
29	TU		29	FR	Black Friday
30	WE		30	SA	
31	TH	Helloween			

DECEMBER

01	SU	
02	MO	Cyber Monday — 49
03	TU	
04	WE	
05	TH	
06	FR	
07	SA	Pearl Harbor Remembrance Day
08	SU	50
09	MO	
10	TU	
11	WE	
12	TH	
13	FR	
14	SA	
15	SU	51
16	MO	
17	TU	
18	WE	
19	TH	
20	FR	
21	SA	
22	SU	52
23	MO	
24	TU	
25	WE	Christmas Day
26	TH	
27	FR	
28	SA	
29	SU	
30	MO	01
31	TU	New Years Eve

JANUARY 2020

01	WE	New Years Day
02	TH	
03	FR	
04	SA	
05	SU	
06	MO	02
07	TU	
08	WE	
09	TH	
10	FR	
11	SA	
12	SU	
13	MO	03
14	TU	
15	WE	
16	TH	
17	FR	
18	SA	
19	SU	
20	MO	Martin Luther King Day — 04
21	TU	
22	WE	
23	TH	
24	FR	Belly Laugh Day
25	SA	
26	SU	
27	MO	05
28	TU	
29	WE	
30	TH	
31	Fr	

FEBRUARY

01	SA	
02	SU	Groundhog Day
03	MO	06
04	TU	
05	WE	
06	TH	
07	FR	
08	SA	
09	SU	
10	MO	07
11	TU	
12	WE	Lincolns Birthday
13	TH	
14	FR	Valentines Day
15	SA	
16	SU	
17	MO	Presidents Day Washingtons Birthday 08
18	TU	
19	WE	
20	TH	
21	FR	
22	SA	
23	SU	
24	MO	09
25	TU	Mardi Grad Carnival
26	WE	
27	TH	
28	Fr	
29	SA	

MARCH

01	SU	
02	MO	10
03	TU	
04	WE	
05	TH	
06	FR	
07	SA	
08	SU	Daylight Saving
09	MO	11
10	TU	
11	WE	
12	TH	
13	FR	
14	SA	
15	SU	
16	MO	12
17	TU	St. Patricks Day
18	WE	
19	TH	
20	FR	
21	SA	
22	SU	
23	MO	13
24	TU	
25	WE	
26	TH	
27	FR	
28	SA	
29	SU	
30	Mo	14
31	TU	

APRIL

01	WE	April Fools Day
02	TH	
03	FR	
04	SA	
05	SU	
06	MO	15
07	TU	
08	WE	
09	TH	
10	FR	Good Friday
11	SA	
12	SU	Easter
13	MO	Easter Monday	16
14	TU	
15	WE	
16	TH	
17	FR	
18	SA	
19	SU	
20	MO	17
21	TU	
22	WE	
23	TH	
24	FR	
25	SA	
26	SU	
27	MO	18
28	TU	
29	WE	
30	TH	

MAY

01	FR	
02	SA	
03	SU	
04	MO	19
05	TU	Cinco De Mayo
06	WE	
07	TH	
08	FR	
09	SA	
10	SU	Mothers Day
11	MO	20
12	TU	
13	WE	
14	TH	
15	FR	
16	SA	Armed Forces Day
17	SU	
18	MO	21
19	TU	
20	WE	
21	TH	
22	FR	
23	SA	
24	SU	
25	MO	Memorial Day	22
26	TU	
27	WE	
28	TH	
29	FR	
30	SA	
31	SU	Pentecost

JUNE				JULY		
01	MO	Pentecost Monday	23	01	WE	
02	TU			02	TH	
03	WE			03	FR	
04	TH			04	SA	Independence Day
05	FR			05	SU	
06	SA			06	MO	28
07	SU			07	TU	
08	MO	24		08	WE	
09	TU			09	TH	
10	WE			10	FR	
11	TH			11	SA	
12	FR			12	SU	
13	SA			13	MO	29
14	SU	Flag Day		14	TU	
15	MO	25		15	WE	
16	TU			16	TH	
17	WE			17	FR	
18	TH			18	SA	
19	FR			19	SU	
20	SA			20	MO	30
21	SU	Fathers Day		21	TU	
22	MO	26		22	WE	
23	TU			23	TH	
24	WE			24	FR	
25	TH			25	SA	
26	FR			26	SU	Parents Day
27	SA			27	MO	31
28	SU			28	TU	
29	MO	27		29	WE	
30	TU			30	TH	
				31	FR	

01	SA	
02	SU	
03	MO	32
04	TU	
05	WE	
06	TH	
07	FR	
08	SA	
09	SU	
10	MO	33
11	TU	
12	WE	
13	TH	
14	FR	
15	SA	
16	SU	
17	MO	34
18	TU	
19	WE	
20	TH	
21	FR	
22	SA	
23	SU	
24	MO	35
25	TU	
26	WE	
27	TH	
28	FR	
29	SA	
30	SU	
31	MO	36

NOTES

TIMETABLE

TIME	MONDAY	TUESDAY	WEDNESDAY

THURSDAY	FRIDAY	SATURDAY	SUNDAY

TIMETABLE

TIME	MONDAY	TUESDAY	WEDNESDAY

THURSDAY	FRIDAY	SATURDAY	SUNDAY

TIMETABLE

TIME	MONDAY	TUESDAY	WEDNESDAY

THURSDAY	FRIDAY	SATURDAY	SUNDAY

JULY 2019

MO	TU	WE	TH	FR	SA	SU
1	2	3	4	5	6	7
8	9	10	11	12	13	14
15	16	17	18	19	20	21
22	23	24	25	26	27	28
29	30	31				

EXAMS

IMPORTANT
APPOINTMENTS

SEPT 2019

MO	TU	WE	TH	FR	SA	SU
						1
2	3	4	5	6	7	8
9	10	11	12	13	14	15
16	17	18	19	20	21	22
23	24	25	26	27	28	29
30						

AUGUST

MONDAY	TUESDAY	WEDNESDAY
29	30	31
5	6	7
12	13	14
19	20	21
26	27	28
2	3	4

2019

THURSDAY	FRIDAY	SATURDAY	SUNDAY
1	2	3	4
8	9	10	11
15	16	17	18
22	23	24	25
29	30	31	1
5	6	7	8

WEEK 31

MONDAY
29
SEPTEMBER

TUESDAY
30
SEPTEMBER

WEDNESDAY
31
SEPTEMBER

THURSDAY
01
SEPTEMBER

FRIDAY

02
SEPTEMBER

☐
☐
☐
☐
☐
☐
☐

SATURDAY

03
SEPTEMBER

☐
☐
☐
☐
☐
☐

SUNDAY

04
SEPTEMBER

☐
☐
☐
☐
☐
☐

WEEK 32

MONDAY
05
SEPTEMBER

TUESDAY
06
SEPTEMBER

WEDNESDAY
07
SEPTEMBER

THURSDAY
08
SEPTEMBER

FRIDAY

09

SEPTEMBER

☐
☐
☐
☐
☐
☐
☐

SATURDAY

10

SEPTEMBER

☐
☐
☐
☐
☐
☐
☐

SUNDAY

11

SEPTEMBER

☐
☐
☐
☐
☐
☐

MONDAY
12
SEPTEMBER

TUESDAY
13
SEPTEMBER

WEDNESDAY
14
SEPTEMBER

THURSDAY
15
SEPTEMBER

FRIDAY

16
SEPTEMBER

☐
☐
☐
☐
☐
☐
☐

SATURDAY

17
SEPTEMBER

☐
☐
☐
☐
☐
☐
☐

SUNDAY

18
SEPTEMBER

☐
☐
☐
☐
☐
☐
☐

MONDAY

19
SEPTEMBER

TUESDAY

20
SEPTEMBER

WEDNESDAY

21
SEPTEMBER

THURSDAY

22
SEPTEMBER

FRIDAY

23

SEPTEMBER

☐
☐
☐
☐
☐
☐
☐

SATURDAY

24

SEPTEMBER

☐
☐
☐
☐
☐
☐
☐

SUNDAY

25

SEPTEMBER

☐
☐
☐
☐
☐
☐
☐

WEEK 35

MONDAY

26
SEPTEMBER

TUESDAY

27
SEPTEMBER

WEDNESDAY

28
SEPTEMBER

THURSDAY

29
SEPTEMBER

FRIDAY

30
SEPTEMBER

☐
☐
☐
☐
☐
☐
☐

SATURDAY

31
SEPTEMBER

☐
☐
☐
☐
☐
☐

SUNDAY

01
SEPTEMBER

☐
☐
☐
☐
☐
☐
☐

AUG 2019

MO	TU	WE	TH	FR	SA	SU
			1	2	3	4
5	6	7	8	9	10	11
12	13	14	15	16	17	18
19	20	21	22	23	24	25
26	27	28	29	30	31	

 EXAMS

 IMPORTANT APPOINTMENTS

OCT 2019

MO	TU	WE	TH	FR	SA	SU
	1	2	3	4	5	6
7	8	9	10	11	12	13
14	15	16	17	18	19	20
21	22	23	24	25	26	27
28	29	30	31			

SEPTEMBER

MONDAY	TUESDAY	WEDNESDAY
26	27	28
2 Labor Day	3	4
9	10	11 Patriot Day
16 Steofamily Day	17 Citizenship Day	18
23	24	25
30	1	2

2019

THURSDAY	FRIDAY	SATURDAY	SUNDAY
29	30	31	1
5	6	7	8 Grandparents Day
12	13	14	15
19	20	21	22
26	27	28	29
3 Native American Day	4	5	6

WEEK 36

MONDAY

Labor Day

02
SEPTEMBER

TUESDAY

03
SEPTEMBER

WEDNESDAY

04
SEPTEMBER

THURSDAY

05
SEPTEMBER

SEPTEMBER 2019

FRIDAY

06
SEPTEMBER

SATURDAY

07
SEPTEMBER

SUNDAY

Grandparents Day

08
SEPTEMBER

MONDAY

09
SEPTEMBER

TUESDAY

10
SEPTEMBER

WEDNESDAY

Patriot Day

11
SEPTEMBER

THURSDAY

12
SEPTEMBER

FRIDAY

13

SEPTEMBER

☐
☐
☐
☐
☐
☐
☐

SATURDAY

14

SEPTEMBER

☐
☐
☐
☐
☐
☐
☐

SUNDAY

15

SEPTEMBER

☐
☐
☐
☐
☐
☐
☐

MONDAY
16
SEPTEMBER

Stepfamily Day

TUESDAY
17
SEPTEMBER

Citizenship Day

WEDNESDAY
18
SEPTEMBER

THURSDAY
19
SEPTEMBER

FRIDAY

20
SEPTEMBER

SATURDAY

21
SEPTEMBER

SUNDAY

22
SEPTEMBER

MONDAY

23
SEPTEMBER

TUESDAY

24
SEPTEMBER

WEDNESDAY

25
SEPTEMBER

THURSDAY

26
SEPTEMBER

FRIDAY

27

SEPTEMBER

Native American Day

- [ ]
- [ ]
- [ ]
- [ ]
- [ ]
- [ ]
- [ ]

SATURDAY

28

SEPTEMBER

- [ ]
- [ ]
- [ ]
- [ ]
- [ ]
- [ ]

SUNDAY

29

SEPTEMBER

- [ ]
- [ ]
- [ ]
- [ ]
- [ ]
- [ ]
- [ ]

SEPT 2019

MO	TU	WE	TH	FR	SA	SU
						1
2	3	4	5	6	7	8
9	10	11	12	13	14	15
16	17	18	19	20	21	22
23	24	25	26	27	28	29
30						

EXAMS

IMPORTANT
APPOINTMENTS

NOV 2019

MO	TU	WE	TH	FR	SA	SU
				1	2	3
4	5	6	7	8	9	10
11	12	13	14	15	16	17
18	19	20	21	22	23	24
25	26	27	28	29	30	

OCTOBER

MONDAY	TUESDAY	WEDNESDAY
30	1	2
7	8	9
14	15	16
Columbus Day		Boss Day
21	22	23
28	29	30

2019

THURSDAY	FRIDAY	SATURDAY	SUNDAY
3	4	5	6
10	11	12	13
17	18	19 Sweetest Day	20
24	25	26	27
31 Halloween	1	2	3

MONDAY

30
SEPTEMBER

☐
☐
☐
☐
☐
☐
☐

TUESDAY

01
OCTOBER

☐
☐
☐
☐
☐
☐
☐

WEDNESDAY

02
OCTOBER

☐
☐
☐
☐
☐
☐
☐

THURSDAY

03
OCTOBER

☐
☐
☐
☐
☐
☐
☐

FRIDAY

04
OCTOBER

SATURDAY

05
OCTOBER

SUNDAY

06
OCTOBER

MONDAY

07

OCTOBER

TUESDAY

08

OCTOBER

WEDNESDAY

09

OCTOBER

THURSDAY

10

OCTOBER

FRIDAY

11

OCTOBER

☐
☐
☐
☐
☐
☐
☐

SATURDAY

12

OCTOBER

☐
☐
☐
☐
☐
☐
☐

SUNDAY

13

OCTOBER

☐
☐
☐
☐
☐
☐
☐

WEEK 42

MONDAY
14
OCTOBER

- [ ]
- [ ]
- [ ]
- [ ]
- [ ]
- [ ]
- [ ]

TUESDAY
15
OCTOBER

- [ ]
- [ ]
- [ ]
- [ ]
- [ ]
- [ ]
- [ ]

WEDNESDAY
16
OCTOBER

Boss Day

- [ ]
- [ ]
- [ ]
- [ ]
- [ ]
- [ ]

THURSDAY
17
OCTOBER

- [ ]
- [ ]
- [ ]
- [ ]
- [ ]
- [ ]
- [ ]

FRIDAY

18
OCTOBER

- [ ]
- [ ]
- [ ]
- [ ]
- [ ]
- [ ]
- [ ]

Sweetest Day

SATURDAY

19
OCTOBER

- [ ]
- [ ]
- [ ]
- [ ]
- [ ]
- [ ]
- [ ]

SUNDAY

20
OCTOBER

- [ ]
- [ ]
- [ ]
- [ ]
- [ ]
- [ ]
- [ ]

MONDAY

21
OCTOBER

TUESDAY

22
OCTOBER

WEDNESDAY

23
OCTOBER

THURSDAY

24
OCTOBER

FRIDAY

25
OCTOBER

SATURDAY

26
OCTOBER

SUNDAY

27
OCTOBER

MONDAY
28
OCTOBER

TUESDAY
29
OCTOBER

WEDNESDAY
30
OCTOBER

THURSDAY
Helloween
31
OCTOBER

FRIDAY

01
NOVEMBER

☐
☐
☐
☐
☐
☐
☐

SATURDAY

02
NOVEMBER

☐
☐
☐
☐
☐
☐
☐

SUNDAY

03
NOVEMBER

Daylight Saving

☐
☐
☐
☐
☐
☐
☐

EXAMS

 IMPORTANT APPOINTMENTS

NOVEMBER

MONDAY	TUESDAY	WEDNESDAY
28	29	30
4	5	6
11	12	13
Veterans Day		
18	19	20
25	26	27

2019

THURSDAY	FRIDAY	SATURDAY	SUNDAY
31	1	2	3 Daylight Saving
7	8	9	10
14	15	16	17
21	22	23	24
28 Thanksgiving	29 Black Friday	30	1

WEEK 45

MONDAY
04
NOVEMBER

TUESDAY
05
NOVEMBER

WEDNESDAY
06
NOVEMBER

THURSDAY
07
NOVEMBER

FRIDAY

08
NOVEMBER

SATURDAY

09
NOVEMBER

SUNDAY

10
NOVEMBER

MONDAY
11
NOVEMBER

Veterans Day

☐
☐
☐
☐
☐
☐
☐

TUESDAY
12
NOVEMBER

☐
☐
☐
☐
☐
☐
☐

WEDNESDAY
13
NOVEMBER

☐
☐
☐
☐
☐
☐

THURSDAY
14
NOVEMBER

☐
☐
☐
☐
☐
☐
☐

FRIDAY

15

NOVEMBER

☐
☐
☐
☐
☐
☐
☐

SATURDAY

16

NOVEMBER

☐
☐
☐
☐
☐
☐
☐

SUNDAY

17

NOVEMBER

☐
☐
☐
☐
☐
☐
☐

WEEK 47

MONDAY

18
NOVEMBER

TUESDAY

19
NOVEMBER

WEDNESDAY

20
NOVEMBER

THURSDAY

21
NOVEMBER

FRIDAY

22
NOVEMBER

☐
☐
☐
☐
☐
☐
☐

SATURDAY

23
NOVEMBER

☐
☐
☐
☐
☐
☐
☐

SUNDAY

24
NOVEMBER

☐
☐
☐
☐
☐
☐
☐

MONDAY
25
NOVEMBER

TUESDAY
26
NOVEMBER

WEDNESDAY
27
NOVEMBER

THURSDAY

Thanksgiving

28
NOVEMBER

FRIDAY

29

NOVEMBER

Black Friday

☐
☐
☐
☐
☐
☐
☐

SATURDAY

30

NOVEMBER

☐
☐
☐
☐
☐
☐

SUNDAY

01

DECEMBER

☐
☐
☐
☐
☐
☐

NOV 2019

MO	TU	WE	TH	FR	SA	SU
				1	2	3
4	5	6	7	8	9	10
11	12	13	14	15	16	17
18	19	20	21	22	23	24
25	26	27	28	29	30	

 EXAMS

■ IMPORTANT APPOINTMENTS

JAN 2020

MO	TU	WE	TH	FR	SA	SU
		1	2	3	4	5
6	7	8	9	10	11	12
13	14	15	16	17	18	19
20	21	22	23	24	25	26
27	28	29	30	31		

DECEMBER

MONDAY	TUESDAY	WEDNESDAY
25	26	27
2 Cyber Monday	3	4
9	10	11
16	17	18
23	24	25 Christmas Day
30	31 New Years Eve	1

2019

THURSDAY	FRIDAY	SATURDAY	SUNDAY
28	29	30	1
5	6	7 Pearl Harbor Rememorance Day	8
12	13	14	15
19	20	21	22
26	27	28	29
2	3	4	5

WEEK 49

MONDAY
02
DECEMBER

Cyoer Monday

- [ ]
- [ ]
- [ ]
- [ ]
- [ ]
- [ ]
- [ ]

TUESDAY
03
DECEMBER

- [ ]
- [ ]
- [ ]
- [ ]
- [ ]
- [ ]
- [ ]

WEDNESDAY
04
DECEMBER

- [ ]
- [ ]
- [ ]
- [ ]
- [ ]
- [ ]
- [ ]

THURSDAY
05
DECEMBER

- [ ]
- [ ]
- [ ]
- [ ]
- [ ]
- [ ]
- [ ]

FRIDAY

06
DECEMBER

☐
☐
☐
☐
☐
☐
☐

SATURDAY

07
DECEMBER

Pearl Harbor Rememorance Day

☐
☐
☐
☐
☐
☐
☐

SUNDAY

08
DECEMBER

☐
☐
☐
☐
☐
☐
☐

MONDAY
09
DECEMBER

TUESDAY
10
DECEMBER

WEDNESDAY
11
DECEMBER

THURSDAY
12
DECEMBER

FRIDAY

13
DECEMBER

SATURDAY

14
DECEMBER

SUNDAY

15
DECEMBER

MONDAY

16
DECEMBER

TUESDAY

17
DECEMBER

WEDNESDAY

18
DECEMBER

THURSDAY

19
DECEMBER

FRIDAY

20

DECEMBER

SATURDAY

21

DECEMBER

SUNDAY

22

DECEMBER

MONDAY

23
DECEMBER

TUESDAY

24
DECEMBER

Christmas Day

WEDNESDAY

25
DECEMBER

THURSDAY

26
DECEMBER

FRIDAY

27
DECEMBER

☐
☐
☐
☐
☐
☐
☐

SATURDAY

28
DECEMBER

☐
☐
☐
☐
☐
☐

SUNDAY

29
DECEMBER

☐
☐
☐
☐
☐
☐
☐

DEC 2019

MO TU WE TH FR SA SU
						1
2	3	4	5	6	7	8
9	10	11	12	13	14	15
16	17	18	19	20	21	22
23	24	25	26	27	28	29
30	31					

 EXAMS

 IMPORTANT APPOINTMENTS

FEB 2020

MO TU WE TH FR SA SU
					1	2
3	4	5	6	7	8	9
10	11	12	13	14	15	16
17	18	19	20	21	22	23
24	25	26	27	28	29	

JANUARY

MONDAY	TUESDAY	WEDNESDAY
30	31	1 New Years Day
6	7	8
13	14	15
20	21	22
Martin Luther King Day		
27	28	29

2020

THURSDAY	FRIDAY	SATURDAY	SUNDAY
2	3	4	5
9	10	11	12
16	17	18	19
23	24 Belly Laugh Day	25	26
30	31	1	2

MONDAY

30
DECEMBER

TUESDAY

New Years Eve

31
DECEMBER

WEDNESDAY

New Years Day

01
JANUARY

THURSDAY

02
JANUARY

FRIDAY

03

JANUARY

SATURDAY

04

JANUARY

SUNDAY

05

JANUARY

MONDAY

06
JANUARY

TUESDAY

07
JANUARY

WEDNESDAY

08
JANUARY

THURSDAY

9
JANUARY

FRIDAY

10
JANUARY

☐
☐
☐
☐
☐
☐
☐

SATURDAY

11
JANUARY

☐
☐
☐
☐
☐
☐
☐

SUNDAY

12
JANUARY

☐
☐
☐
☐
☐
☐
☐

MONDAY

13

JANUARY

TUESDAY

14

JANUARY

WEDNESDAY

15

JANUARY

THURSDAY

16

JANUARY

FRIDAY

17
JANUARY

SATURDAY

18
JANUARY

SUNDAY

19
JANUARY

WEEK 04

MONDAY
20
JANUARY

Martin Luther King Day

TUESDAY
21
JANUARY

WEDNESDAY
22
JANUARY

THURSDAY
23
JANUARY

FRIDAY

24
JANUARY

Belly Laugh Day

☐
☐
☐
☐
☐
☐
☐

SATURDAY

25
JANUARY

☐
☐
☐
☐
☐
☐
☐

SUNDAY

26
JANUARY

☐
☐
☐
☐
☐
☐
☐

MONDAY

27

JANUARY

TUESDAY

28

JANUARY

WEDNESDAY

29

JANUARY

THURSDAY

30

JANUARY

FRIDAY

31
JANUARY

- [ ]
- [ ]
- [ ]
- [ ]
- [ ]
- [ ]
- [ ]

SATURDAY

01
FEBRUARY

- [ ]
- [ ]
- [ ]
- [ ]
- [ ]
- [ ]
- [ ]

SUNDAY

02
FEBRUARY

Groundhog Day

- [ ]
- [ ]
- [ ]
- [ ]
- [ ]
- [ ]
- [ ]

JAN 2020

MO TU WE TH FR SA SU
            1 2 3 4 5
6 7 8 9 10 11 12
13 14 15 16 17 18 19
20 21 22 23 24 25 26
27 28 29 30 31

 EXAMS

 IMPORTANT
APPOINTMENTS

MAR 2020

MO TU WE TH FR SA SU
                     1
2 3 4 5 6 7 8
9 10 11 12 13 14 15
16 17 18 19 20 21 22
23 24 25 26 27 28 29
30 31

FEBRUARY

MONDAY	TUESDAY	WEDNESDAY
26	27	28
3	4	5
10	11	12 Lincolns Birthday
17 Presidents Day Washintons Birthday	18	19
24	25 Mardi Grad Carnival	26

2020

THURSDAY	FRIDAY	SATURDAY	SUNDAY
29	30	1	2 Groundhog Day
6	7	8	9
13	14 Valentines Day	15	16
20	21	22	23
27	28	29	1

MONDAY

03
FEBRUARY

TUESDAY

04
FEBRUARY

WEDNESDAY

05
FEBRUARY

THURSDAY

06
FEBRUARY

FRIDAY

07
FEBRUARY

☐
☐
☐
☐
☐
☐
☐

SATURDAY

08
FEBRUARY

☐
☐
☐
☐
☐
☐
☐

SUNDAY

09
FEBRUARY

☐
☐
☐
☐
☐
☐
☐

MONDAY

10
FEBRUARY

TUESDAY

11
FEBRUARY

WEDNESDAY

Lincolns Birthday

12
FEBRUARY

THURSDAY

13
FEBRUARY

Valentines Day

FRIDAY

14

FEBRUARY

☐
☐
☐
☐
☐
☐
☐

SATURDAY

15

FEBRUARY

☐
☐
☐
☐
☐
☐
☐

SUNDAY

16

FEBRUARY

☐
☐
☐
☐
☐
☐
☐

MONDAY

17
FEBRUARY

Presidents Day & Washintons Birthday

TUESDAY

18
FEBRUARY

WEDNESDAY

19
FEBRUARY

THURSDAY

20
FEBRUARY

FRIDAY

21
FEBRUARY

☐
☐
☐
☐
☐
☐
☐

SATURDAY

22
FEBRUARY

☐
☐
☐
☐
☐
☐
☐

SUNDAY

23
FEBRUARY

☐
☐
☐
☐
☐
☐
☐

MONDAY

24

FEBRUARY

TUESDAY

Mardi Grad Carnival

25

FEBRUARY

WEDNESDAY

26

FEBRUARY

THURSDAY

27

FEBRUARY

FRIDAY

28
FEBRUARY

☐
☐
☐
☐
☐
☐
☐

SATURDAY

29
FEBRUARY

☐
☐
☐
☐
☐
☐

SUNDAY

01
MARCH

☐
☐
☐
☐
☐
☐

FEB 2020

MO	TU	WE	TH	FR	SA	SU
					1	2
3	4	5	6	7	8	9
10	11	12	13	14	15	16
17	18	19	20	21	22	23
24	25	26	27	28	29	

 EXAMS

IMPORTANT
APPOINTMENTS

APR 2020

MO	TU	WE	TH	FR	SA	SU
		1	2	3	4	5
6	7	8	9	10	11	12
13	14	15	16	17	18	19
20	21	22	23	24	25	26
27	28	29	30			

MARCH

MONDAY	TUESDAY	WEDNESDAY
24	25	26
2	3	4
9	10	11
16	17	18
	St- Patricks Day	
23	24	25
30	31	

2020

THURSDAY	FRIDAY	SATURDAY	SUNDAY
27	28	29	1
5	6	7	8 Daylight Saving
12	13	14	15
19	20	21	22
26	27	28	29

MONDAY

02
MARCH

TUESDAY

03
MARCH

WEDNESDAY

04
MARCH

THURSDAY

05
MARCH

FRIDAY

06
MARCH

☐
☐
☐
☐
☐
☐

SATURDAY

07
MARCH

☐
☐
☐
☐
☐
☐
☐

SUNDAY

08
MARCH

Daylight Saving

☐
☐
☐
☐
☐
☐
☐

MONDAY

09

MARCH

☐
☐
☐
☐
☐
☐
☐

TUESDAY

10

MARCH

☐
☐
☐
☐
☐
☐
☐

WEDNESDAY

11

MARCH

☐
☐
☐
☐
☐
☐
☐

THURSDAY

12

MARCH

☐
☐
☐
☐
☐
☐
☐

FRIDAY

13
MARCH

SATURDAY

14
MARCH

SUNDAY

15
MARCH

WEEK 12

MONDAY
16
MARCH

TUESDAY
17
MARCH

St- Patricks Day

WEDNESDAY
18
MARCH

THURSDAY
19
MARCH

FRIDAY

20

MARCH

☐
☐
☐
☐
☐
☐
☐

SATURDAY

21

MARCH

☐
☐
☐
☐
☐
☐
☐
☐

SUNDAY

22

MARCH

☐
☐
☐
☐
☐
☐
☐

MONDAY

23
MARCH

TUESDAY

24
MARCH

WEDNESDAY

25
MARCH

THURSDAY

26
MARCH

FRIDAY

27
MARCH

☐
☐
☐
☐
☐
☐

SATURDAY

28
MARCH

☐
☐
☐
☐
☐
☐

SUNDAY

29
MARCH

☐
☐
☐
☐
☐
☐

EXAMS

 IMPORTANT APPOINTMENTS

APRIL

MONDAY	TUESDAY	WEDNESDAY
30	31	1 April Fools Day
6	7	8
13	14	15
20 Easter Monday	21	22
27	28	29

2020

THURSDAY	FRIDAY	SATURDAY	SUNDAY
2	3	4	5
9	10 Good Friday	11	12 Easter
16	17	18	19
23	24	25	26
30	1	2	3

MONDAY

30
MARCH

TUESDAY

31
MARCH

WEDNESDAY

Aoril Fools Day

01
APRIL

THURSDAY

02
APRIL

FRIDAY

03
APRIL

SATURDAY

04
APRIL

SUNDAY

05
APRIL

MONDAY
06
APRIL

TUESDAY
07
APRIL

WEDNESDAY
08
APRIL

THURSDAY
09
APRIL

FRIDAY

10
APRIL

Good Friday

SATURDAY

11
APRIL

SUNDAY

12
APRIL

Easter

MONDAY

Easter Monday

13
APRIL

TUESDAY

14
APRIL

WEDNESDAY

15
APRIL

THURSDAY

16
APRIL

FRIDAY

17
APRIL

SATURDAY

18
APRIL

SUNDAY

19
APRIL

MONDAY
20
APRIL

TUESDAY
21
APRIL

WEDNESDAY
22
APRIL

THURSDAY
23
APRIL

FRIDAY

24
APRIL

SATURDAY

25
APRIL

SUNDAY

26
APRIL

WEEK 18

MONDAY
27
APRIL

TUESDAY
28
APRIL

WEDNESDAY
29
APRIL

THURSDAY
30
APRIL

FRIDAY

01
MAY

☐
☐
☐
☐
☐
☐
☐

SATURDAY

02
MAY

☐
☐
☐
☐
☐
☐
☐

SUNDAY

03
MAY

☐
☐
☐
☐
☐
☐
☐

APR 2020

MO TU WE TH FR SA SU

　　　　1　2　3　4　5
6　7　8　9　10　11　12
13　14　15　16　17　18　19
20　21　22　23　24　25　26
27　28　29　30

 EXAMS

IMPORTANT
APPOINTMENTS

JUN 2020

MO TU WE TH FR SA SU

1　2　3　4　5　6　7
8　9　10　11　12　13　14
15　16　17　18　19　20　21
22　23　24　25　26　27　28
29　30

MAY

MONDAY	TUESDAY	WEDNESDAY
27	28	29
4	5 Cinco De Mayo	6
11	12	13
18	19	20
25 Memorial Day	26	27

2020

THURSDAY	FRIDAY	SATURDAY	SUNDAY
30	1	2	3
7	8	9	10 Mothers Day
14	15	16 Armed Forces Day	17
21	22	23	24
28	29	30	31 Pentecost

MONDAY
04
MAY

TUESDAY
05
MAY

Cinco De Mayo

WEDNESDAY
06
MAY

THURSDAY
07
MAY

FRIDAY

08
MAY

☐
☐
☐
☐
☐
☐
☐

SATURDAY

09
MAY

☐
☐
☐
☐
☐
☐
☐

SUNDAY

10
MAY

Mother's Day

☐
☐
☐
☐
☐
☐
☐

MONDAY

11
MAY

TUESDAY

12
MAY

WEDNESDAY

13
MAY

THURSDAY

14
MAY

FRIDAY

15
MAY

☐
☐
☐
☐
☐
☐
☐

Armed Forces Day

SATURDAY

16
MAY

☐
☐
☐
☐
☐
☐
☐

SUNDAY

17
MAY

☐
☐
☐
☐
☐
☐
☐

MONDAY

18
MAY

TUESDAY

19
MAY

WEDNESDAY

20
MAY

THURSDAY

21
MAY

FRIDAY

22
MAY

SATURDAY

23
MAY

SUNDAY

24
MAY

MONDAY

Memorial Day

25
MAY

TUESDAY

26
MAY

WEDNESDAY

27
MAY

THURSDAY

28
MAY

FRIDAY

29
MAY

SATURDAY

30
MAY

SUNDAY

Pentecost

31
MAY

MAY 2020

MO	TU	WE	TH	FR	SA	SU
				1	2	3
4	5	6	7	8	9	10
11	12	13	14	15	16	17
18	19	20	21	22	23	24
25	26	27	28	29	30	31

 EXAMS

 IMPORTANT APPOINTMENTS

JUL 2020

MO	TU	WE	TH	FR	SA	SU
	1	2	3	4	5	
6	7	8	9	10	11	12
13	14	15	16	17	18	19
20	21	22	23	24	25	26
27	28	29	30	31		

JUNE

MONDAY	TUESDAY	WEDNESDAY
1 Pentecost Monday	2	3
8	9	10
15	16	17
22	23	24
29	30	1

2020

THURSDAY	FRIDAY	SATURDAY	SUNDAY
4	5	6	7
11	12	13	14 Flag Day
18	19	20	21 Father's Day
25	26	27	28
2	3	4	5

WEEK 23

MONDAY
01
JUNE

Pentecost Monday

- [ ]
- [ ]
- [ ]
- [ ]
- [ ]
- [ ]
- [ ]

TUESDAY
02
JUNE

- [ ]
- [ ]
- [ ]
- [ ]
- [ ]
- [ ]
- [ ]

WEDNESDAY
03
JUNE

- [ ]
- [ ]
- [ ]
- [ ]
- [ ]
- [ ]

THURSDAY
04
JUNE

- [ ]
- [ ]
- [ ]
- [ ]
- [ ]
- [ ]
- [ ]

FRIDAY

05
JUNE

SATURDAY

06
JUNE

SUNDAY

07
JUNE

WEEK 24

MONDAY
08
JUNE

TUESDAY
09
JUNE

WEDNESDAY
10
JUNE

THURSDAY
11
JUNE

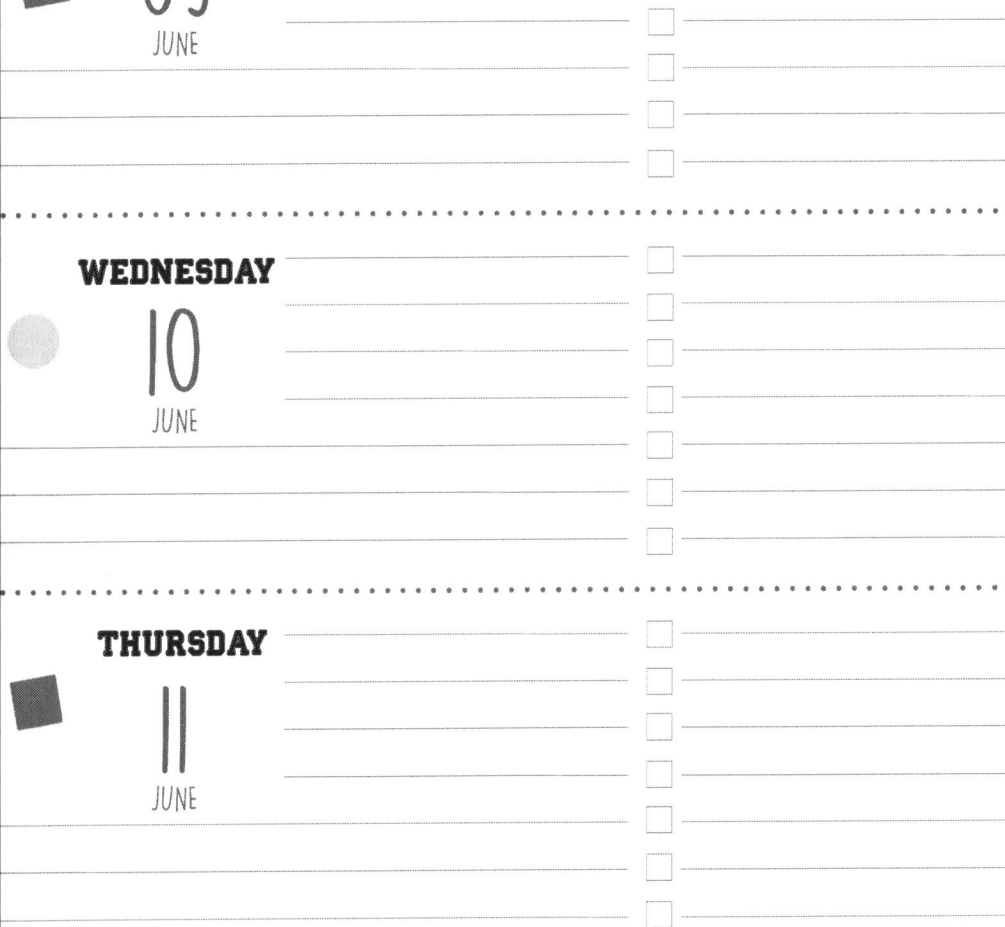

FRIDAY

12
JUNE

- [ ]
- [ ]
- [ ]
- [ ]
- [ ]
- [ ]
- [ ]

SATURDAY

13
JUNE

- [ ]
- [ ]
- [ ]
- [ ]
- [ ]
- [ ]
- [ ]

SUNDAY

14
JUNE

Flag Day

- [ ]
- [ ]
- [ ]
- [ ]
- [ ]
- [ ]
- [ ]

MONDAY

15
JUNE

TUESDAY

16
JUNE

WEDNESDAY

17
JUNE

THURSDAY

18
JUNE

FRIDAY

19
JUNE

☐
☐
☐
☐
☐
☐
☐

SATURDAY

20
JUNE

☐
☐
☐
☐
☐
☐
☐

SUNDAY

21
JUNE

Fathers Day

☐
☐
☐
☐
☐
☐

MONDAY
22
JUNE

TUESDAY
23
JUNE

WEDNESDAY
24
JUNE

THURSDAY
25
JUNE

FRIDAY

26
JUNE

☐
☐
☐
☐
☐
☐
☐

SATURDAY

27
JUNE

☐
☐
☐
☐
☐
☐
☐

SUNDAY

28
JUNE

☐
☐
☐
☐
☐
☐
☐

WEEK 27

MONDAY

29
JUNE

TUESDAY

30
JUNE

WEDNESDAY

01
JULY

THURSDAY

02
JULY

JUNE - JULY 2020

FRIDAY

03
JULY

- [ ]
- [ ]
- [ ]
- [ ]
- [ ]
- [ ]
- [ ]

SATURDAY

04
JULY

Independence Day

- [ ]
- [ ]
- [ ]
- [ ]
- [ ]
- [ ]

SUNDAY

05
JULY

- [ ]
- [ ]
- [ ]
- [ ]
- [ ]
- [ ]

JUN 2020

MO TU WE TH FR SA SU

MO	TU	WE	TH	FR	SA	SU
1	2	3	4	5	6	7
8	9	10	11	12	13	14
15	16	17	18	19	20	21
22	23	24	25	26	27	28
29	30					

 EXAMS

 IMPORTANT APPOINTMENTS

AUG 2020

MO TU WE TH FR SA SU

MO	TU	WE	TH	FR	SA	SU
					1	2
3	4	5	6	7	8	9
10	11	12	13	14	15	16
17	18	19	20	21	22	23
24	25	26	27	28	29	30
31						

JULY

MONDAY	TUESDAY	WEDNESDAY
29	30	1
6	7	8
13	14	15
20	21	22
27	28	29

2020

THURSDAY	FRIDAY	SATURDAY	SUNDAY
2	3	4 Independence Day	5
9	10	11	12
16	17	18	19
23	24	25	26 Parents Day
30	31	1	2

MONDAY
06
JULY

TUESDAY
07
JULY

WEDNESDAY
08
JULY

THURSDAY
09
JULY

FRIDAY

10
JULY

☐
☐
☐
☐
☐
☐

SATURDAY

11
JULY

☐
☐
☐
☐
☐
☐

SUNDAY

12
JULY

☐
☐
☐
☐
☐
☐

MONDAY

13

JULY

TUESDAY

14

JULY

WEDNESDAY

15

JULY

THURSDAY

16

JULY

FRIDAY

17
JULY

SATURDAY

18
JULY

SUNDAY

19
JULY

WEEK 30

MONDAY
20
JULY

TUESDAY
21
JULY

WEDNESDAY
22
JULY

THURSDAY
23
JULY

FRIDAY

24
JULY

- [ ]
- [ ]
- [ ]
- [ ]
- [ ]
- [ ]
- [ ]

SATURDAY

25
JULY

- [ ]
- [ ]
- [ ]
- [ ]
- [ ]
- [ ]
- [ ]

SUNDAY

26
JULY

Parents Day

- [ ]
- [ ]
- [ ]
- [ ]
- [ ]
- [ ]
- [ ]

MONDAY

27

JULY

TUESDAY

28

JULY

WEDNESDAY

29

JULY

THURSDAY

30

JULY

FRIDAY

31
JULY

SATURDAY

01
AUGUST

SUNDAY

02
AUGUST

NOTES

JAN 2021

MO	TU	WE	TH	FR	SA	SU
				1	2	3
4	5	6	7	8	9	10
11	12	13	14	15	16	17
18	19	20	21	22	23	24
25	26	27	28	29	30	31

FEB 2021

MO	TU	WE	TH	FR	SA	SU
1	2	3	4	5	6	7
8	9	10	11	12	13	14
15	16	17	18	19	20	21
22	23	24	25	26	27	28

MAR 2021

MO	TU	WE	TH	FR	SA	SU
1	2	3	4	5	6	7
8	9	10	11	12	13	14
15	16	17	18	19	20	21
22	23	24	25	26	27	28
29	30	31				

APR 2021

MO	TU	WE	TH	FR	SA	SU
			1	2	3	4
5	6	7	8	9	10	11
12	13	14	15	16	17	18
19	20	21	22	23	24	25
26	27	28	29	30		

MAY 2021

MO	TU	WE	TH	FR	SA	SU
					1	2
3	4	5	6	7	8	9
10	11	12	13	14	15	16
17	18	19	20	21	22	23
24	25	26	27	28	29	30
31						

JUN 2021

MO	TU	WE	TH	FR	SA	SU
	1	2	3	4	5	6
7	8	9	10	11	12	13
14	15	16	17	18	19	20
21	22	23	24	25	26	27
28	29	30				

JUL 2021

MO	TU	WE	TH	FR	SA	SU
			1	2	3	4
5	6	7	8	9	10	11
12	13	14	15	16	17	18
19	20	21	22	23	24	25
26	27	28	29	30	31	

AUG 2021

MO	TU	WE	TH	FR	SA	SU
						1
2	3	4	5	6	7	8
9	10	11	12	13	14	15
16	17	18	19	20	21	22
23	24	25	26	27	28	29
30	31					

SEPT 2021

MO	TU	WE	TH	FR	SA	SU
		1	2	3	4	5
6	7	8	9	10	11	12
13	14	15	16	17	18	19
20	21	22	23	24	25	26
27	28	29	30			

OCT 2021

MO	TU	WE	TH	FR	SA	SU
				1	2	3
4	5	6	7	8	9	10
11	12	13	14	15	16	17
18	19	20	21	22	23	24
25	26	27	28	29	30	31

NOV 2021

MO	TU	WE	TH	FR	SA	SU
1	2	3	4	5	6	7
8	9	10	11	12	13	14
15	16	17	18	19	20	21
22	23	24	25	26	27	28
29	30					

DEC 2021

MO	TU	WE	TH	FR	SA	SU
		1	2	3	4	5
6	7	8	9	10	11	12
13	14	15	16	17	18	19
20	21	22	23	24	25	26
27	28	29	30	31		

HOLIDAY USA 2019

01.	January	NewYear'sDay
21.	January	MartinLutherKingDay
24.	January	BellyLaughDay
02.	February	GroundhogDay
12.	February	Lincoln'sBirthday
14.	February	Valentine'sDay
18.	February	PresidentsDayAnd Washington'sBirthday
05.	March	MardiGradCarnival
10.	March	DaylightSaving
17.	March	St.Patrick'sDay
01.	April	AprilFool'sDay
19.	April	GoodFriday
21.	April	Easter
22.	April	EasterMonday
05.	May	CincoDeMayo
12.	May	Mother'sDay
18.	May	ArmedForcesDay
27.	May	MemorialDay
09.	June	Pentecost
10.	June	PentecostMonday
14.	June	FlagDay
16.	June	Father'sDay
04.	July	IndependenceDay
28.	July	Parents'Day
02.	September	LaborDay
08.	September	Grandparents'Day
11.	September	PatriotDay September 11th
16.	September	StepfamilyDay
17.	September	CitizenshipDay
27.	September	NativeAmericanDay
14.	October	ColumbusDay
16.	October	Boss'sDay
19.	October	SweetestDay
31.	October	Helloween
03.	November	DaylightSaving
11.	November	Veterans'Day
28.	November	Thanksgiving
29.	November	BlackFriday
02.	December	CyberMonday
07.	December	PearlHarborRemembranceDay
25.	December	ChristmasDay
31.	December	NewYear'sEve

HOLIDAY USA 2020

01.	January	New Year's Day
20.	January	Martin Luther King Day
24.	January	Belly Laugh Day
02.	February	Groundhog Day
12.	February	Lincoln's Birthday
14.	February	Valentine's Day
17.	February	Presidents Day And Washington's Birthday
25.	February	Mardi Grad Carnival
08.	March	Daylight Saving
17.	March	St. Patrick's Day
01.	April	April Fool's Day
10.	April	Good Friday
12.	April	Easter
13.	April	Easter Monday
05.	May	Cinco De Mayo
10.	May	Mother's Day
16.	May	Armed Forces Day
25.	May	Memorial Day
31.	May	Pentecost
01.	June	Pentecost Monday
14.	June	Flag Day
21.	June	Father's Day
04.	July	Independence Day
26.	July	Parents' Day
07.	September	Labor Day
11.	September	Patriot Day September 11th
13.	September	Grandparents' Day
16.	September	Stepfamily Day
17.	September	Citizenship Day
25.	September	Native American Day
12.	October	Columbus Day
16.	October	Boss's Day
17.	October	Sweetest Day
31.	October	Helloween
01.	November	Daylight Saving
11.	November	Veterans' Day
26.	November	Thanksgiving
27.	November	Black Friday
30.	November	Cyber Monday
07.	December	Pearl Harbor Remembrance Day
25.	December	Christmas Day
31.	December	New Year's Eve

Bei Fragen & Anregungen:
feedback@mertens-publication.de

1. Auflage

2018 Mertens Verlagsgruppe

Mertens Ventures Ltd.
Tefkrou Anthia No 2
Office 301
6045 Larnaca
Zypern

E-Maill: kontakt@mertens-publication.de

Printed in Great Britain
by Amazon